MEHREGAAN: THE TRIUMPH OF LIBERTY OVER TYRANNY

MEHREGAAN: THE TRIUMPH OF LIBERTY OVER TYRANNY

DR. KHODADAD (KHODI) KAVIANI

Published in the United States by CreateSpace

Copyright ©2017 Dr. Khodadad (Khodi) Kaviani
All rights reserved.

ISBN-13: 9780692892794
ISBN-10: 0692892796

جشن مهرگان بر همگان خجسته باد!
Merry Mehregaan to All!

ACKNOWLEDGEMENTS

Thank you, Soumen Sarkar, for turning my rough sketches into beautiful illustrations for this story.

I am also thankful to Haideh Esfahani, Michelle Rostami, Mehra Park, Jai Park, and Neema Rostami for their early review of the manuscript and helpful suggestions.

I extend my gratitude to Dr. Roger Soder and Dr. Walter Parker for introducing me to American ideas of leadership and democratic education during my graduate work at University of Washington.

I am grateful to Central Washington University for awarding the sabbatical leave that allowed me to produce this work, and my colleagues for their support.

This book is dedicated to all who have struggled to establish liberty and justice for all, and promote common good in our world.

INTRODUCTION

This work represents my attempt at introducing English language readers to an aspect of Iranian culture that is thought provoking and inspiring. The ancient Iranians had their own interpretation of democracy and knew about the required conditions for sustaining political stability. Democracy is a system of government in which the people are sovereign and rule of law protects them as they participate in civic life of their community. The Greek historian Xenophon wrote about some of these conditions in his book: *Education of Cyrus*. The ancient Iranians had different names and symbols for deities that represented fair rule and public consent.

There are many similarities among those ancient Iranian ideals and modern standards of democratic rule, today. For example, the great seal of the United States shows an eagle holding an olive branch in its right talon, and thirteen arrows in its left talon representing the 13 original states. The olive branch is associated with peace. Similarly, in Iranian culture, lotus flower is used to represent peace, perfection, and harmony. We find the bull-head mace to be equivalent to the arrows held by the eagle's talons, representing war as a last resort when defending the homeland against aggressors. The ring held by the deity Mehr symbolizes the bond between king and people. This fragile bond should be unbreakable; but legends and historical records indicate otherwise. Throughout history, dictators and autocrats have abused power for their personal gains. The ring symbolizes king's commitment to protecting the public and working for common good. In this context, king is a trusted public servant working for prosperity and freedom of the inhabitants.

I have introduced a few fictional characters engaged in conversations to help tell the epic story of metalsmith Kaaveh to a younger generation. Kaaveh was courageous in refusing to go along with the social norms of his time that demanded submission to the will of a monster king who had absolute power over their lives. His occupation as a metalworker represents his toughness and resolve in molding raw metals and shaping them into useful tools. Kaaveh is an accidental leader who finds the courage to speak truth to power, and later, leads the masses to their freedom. Other layers of the story remind us to carefully scrutinize all political candidates and rely on rational mind when electing political leaders. This story serves as a warning to not fall for smooth-talking individuals who make empty promises and fail to protect the general welfare. The story also shows how hard it is to get rid of dictators.

I have used a few modern concept labels to indicate the timeless connections between democracy today and this Iranian legend. The ancient Iranians knew justice and had deities representing it. For example, Mehr, Shahrivar, and Rashn are just three of such deities that provide an initial template for good governance. Mehr reminds people to keep their commitments and be truthful. Nothing is hidden from Mehr's 1000 ears and 10,000 eyes! The 16th day of the month is called Mehr. Shahrivar is about strong leadership for and with justice. The 4th day of the month is called Shahrivar. Rashn treats everyone fairly and does not let class or wealth influence his decisions. Rashn means *Just*, and is the name for 18th day of the month. Transparency in government actions, upholding the just laws, and protecting people are among the ideals that democratic societies have successfully incorporated into their body politic. Safeguarding and promoting the general welfare of people require constant vigilance by community members.

Every Iranian knows the story of Kaaveh. My fascination with Shahnaameh began at a young age when I heard my dad reciting a few of his favorite poems when he wanted to make a point or encourage his children to do something. Using poetry in everyday conversation was a usual practice when I was growing up. It is a common belief among Iranians that Ferdowsi's Shahnaameh is responsible for preserving the Persian language and Iranian identity. Abol-ghaasem Mansoor bin Hassan, known as Ferdowsi Toosi, was born about 1,073 years ago, in the district of Baazh, city of Toos in Khoraasaan. His tomb, in the city of Toos, is an Iranian national monument and a source of pride for all Persian speakers in countries like Afghanistan, Pakistan, Tajikistan and others.

Ferdowsi continued the work of Abu Mansoor Mohammad bin Ahmad Toosi, known as Daghighi, a young poet in the Samanid court. Daghighi's life was cut short about 1,040 years ago when he was murdered. Based on Daghighi's poems, he considered himself to be a Zoroastrian. He argued, when Iranians learned about their ancestral roots and studied the literature, they ended up seeking Zoroaster's path. Zoroaster or Zartosht was an Iranian prophet who believed in AhuraMazdaa (Life Giving Great Wise One). His monotheism influenced Christianity, Judaism, and Islam. Daghighi relied on an earlier collection of poems written by four Zoroastrians from Herat, Seestaan, Shaapoor, and Toos. They wrote for the ruler of Toos, Abu Mansoor Mohammad bin Abdol-razzaagh. This collection of poems is known as Shahnaameh Abu Mansoori. To better understand the historical context, it is necessary to examine the events of that period. However, such thorough examination is beyond the scope of this introduction. Suffice to say, by Ferdowsi's time, more than 300 years had passed since the collapse of the Sassanid dynasty and Iran was under Muslim rule. Books and articles written in Pahlavi language were mostly destroyed and efforts were made to preserve and assert an Iranian identity, separate from the new imported culture that was determined to replace the Zoroastrian traditions. In this context, Shahnaameh was a powerful sign of cultural struggle to preserve what was left of an Iranian identity.

The stories of Shahnaameh are about myths, legends, and history of Iran. In general, a legend is an almost believable story with powerful symbolism for the culture it represents. On the other hand, a myth is an effective form of storytelling that explains ideas that are symbolic and hard to explain. Shahnaameh begins with the roots of Iranian civilization and ends with the fall of Yazdgerd II, the last Sassanid king. Shahnaameh reflects the complex human nature and our lofty aspirations, along with shortcomings and successes in governance and personal relationships. For a book that was written over a thousand years ago, readers can find relevance to their lives, and learn from parables when studying history.

ADDITIONAL READINGS AND RESOURCES

For Shahnaameh (Book of Kings), there are several online resources. A few of them are listed below:

(IN PERSIAN)

http://shahnameh.eu/

http://www.loc.gov/exhibits/thousand-years-of-the-persian-book/epic-of-shahnameh.html

https://www.youtube.com/watch?v=KrBTtKR9Occ

(IN ENGLISH)

http://www.academia.edu/4612436/Translations_of_Shahnameh_of_Firdausi_in_the_West

https://www.sattor.com/Shohnomanakshunigor.html

http://shahnameh-audio.com/home/ (Dr. Afshin Sepehri and his daughter Nusha)

http://www.heritageinstitute.com/zoroastrianism/shahnameh/

http://classics.mit.edu/Ferdowsi/kings.html

Doost-khaah, Jalil (Ed.). (1375 Khorshidi). *Avestaa: Kohantareen Sorood-haaye Eeraaneeyaan* (Vol. 1). Tehran: Enteshaaraat-e Morvaareed.

Oshidari, Jahangir. (1371 Khorshidi). *Daaneshnaameh Mazdayasnaa: Vajheh naameh toozeehee aaeen-e Zartosht* (1st ed.). Tehran: Nashr-e Markaz.

Parker, Walter C. (2003). *Teaching democracy: unity and diversity in public life.* New York: Teachers College Press.

Soder, Roger. (2001). Education for democracy. In R. Soder, John I. Goodlad & Timothy J. McMannon (Eds.), *Developing democratic character in the young* (pp. 184-205). San Francisco: Jossey-Bass.

Soder, Roger (2001). *The language of leadership*. San Francisco: Jossey-Bass.

GLOSSARY

Aabteen: Fereidoon's father. He was killed by Zah-haak's soldiers to feed his snakes. His lineage is connected to King Tahmoores, a mythical king who subdued the forces that were making Iran unsecure. The defeated side asked for Tahmoores's mercy in exchange for teaching him reading, writing, and many other skills.

Azhidahaak = Zah-haak: A devil with ten bad characters that lives in mountains. In Shahnaameh (Book of Kings), Zah-haak is described as a foreign dictator (from ancient Babylon) and an enemy of people, and Iran. According to Aabaan Yasht, Azhidahaak's goal was elimination of all people from the earth. Since he ruled using violence and terror, Azhidahaak represents war, ignorance and dictatorship. If he is not jailed, he would destroy all humanity.

Gorz-e Gaav-meesh Sar = Bull-Head Mace: Wild Water Buffalo Mace: Fereidoon asked for a mace to fight against Zah-haak. The local metalsmiths made him a metal mace in the shape of a bull head with two horns. Fereidoon fought Zah-haak using this weapon, and later the bull-head mace became Fereidoon's family emblem.

Damaavand: This mountain is located in northeast of Tehran, Iran, and is part of the Alborz mountain ranges. Damaavand means *having steam*. This special mountain is where Zah-haak was jailed. According to the legend, he is still there because on occasion, people hear noises coming from this formerly active volcanic mountain.

Divine Blessing = Farreh Eezadee: Farreh is the special light, glory, and strength given to a prophet or leader. People who are blessed with Farreh must remain grateful, just, kind, and work for the people. There are two types of Farreh: (1) Farr-e Eeraani (Iranian Farreh), and (2) Farr-e Keeyaani. According to Ashtaad Yasht, Farr-e Eeraani brings cattle and rich wealth to Iranians and gives knowledge, clear thinking, and good government. This Farreh belongs to Iranians and stays with Iran until the Judgment Day. Farreh Keeyaani is given to competent and honest leaders and rulers.

Enlightened Political Engagement: "Wise participation in public affairs" through peaceful actions, using reason, and collaborative means to find the best solutions to societal problems. For an in-depth explanation of this complex idea, read *Teaching Democracy*, by Walter C. Parker. Please see the reference section.

Faraanak: Fereidoon's mother who became a single mom after Zah-haak's soldiers killed her husband Aabteen.

Fereidoon: When he became 16 years old, he came down the Alborz Mountain and asked his mom about his family's heritage. After learning what happened to his father, he became determined to fight Zah-haak. He joined the movement that Kaaveh began, and chased Zah-haak's forces all the way to Bethlehem. After defeating him, Fereidoon jailed Zah-haak at Damaavand Mountain for eternity.

Father Time: A fictional character I created to narrate the story when needed.

Frenemy: An enemy pretending to be a friend.

Inquiry: A scientific approach used to investigate issues, using credible and reliable sources.

Jamsheed: Son of Tahmoores, he is an inventor of various civilian and military tools. For the first 300 years of his rule, there were no diseases and deaths. He was truthful, humble, and honest. He organized society based on the work they performed. Beginning of the spring season, he celebrated the first Norooz, which is the Iranian New Year. Later on in his rule, he became arrogant and claimed a stature equal to God. Consequently, Farreh Eezadee (Divine Blessing) left him in the shape of a bird flying away. He lost the people's support and this collapse of confidence in his rule paved the way for Zah-haak's entry into Iran.

Justice: Treating people fairly and reasonably under the law.

Kaaveh Aahangar = Metalsmith Kaaveh: When his son was taken away to become snake food for Zah-haak's snakes, he went to Zah-haak's court and pleaded for his son's release. Unlike the others who had signed the petition claiming Zah-haak was a just king, he ripped that petition in half and questioned the king's legitimacy. This was a daring move that stunned the audience present at the royal court! After leaving the court with his son, he put his leather apron on a long lance and rallied people to join Fereidoon. This event marked the beginning of the uprising against Zah-haak.

Kaviani Flag = Derafsh-e Kaaveeyaanee: Kaaveh's apron that he put on a lance to rally people for Fereidoon. His leather apron was decorated with precious jewels and metals, making the flag glow even in the dark. Yellow, red, and purple are the colors associated with this royal standard. The Kaviani Flag signifies courage and victory! This special flag was carried in front of the troops by special standard bearers who wore golden color shoes.

Lotus: This flower has been used to decorate the walls of Persepolis, the massive building representing the might of the Persian Empire. White lotus is a symbol of purity, fortune, and the sun. This flower is held by kings and other nobles.

Mardaas: Father of Zah-haak. Mardaas was known for his generosity and just treatment of others. He had hundreds of horses, goats, camels, and other animals. One night when Mardaas went on his nightly stroll in his garden, he fell into a hole that Zah-haak had dug. Mardaas died and his son, Zah-haak, became the new king.

Sweet Marjoram: A symbol of happiness, this hardy perennial is used for seasoning food.

Mehr = Mitraa = Mithra = Mitra: The guardian of promises and commitments; and the guardian of light and brightness. Zoroastrians call their fire temples, *Dar-e Mehr*, which means *Door of Mehr* (*Gate of Kindness*). Mehr is believed to be strong and always alert. Mehr knows all who on this earth honor or break their promises. According to Mehr Yasht, AhuraMazdaa (Life Giving Wise One = Creator) told Zartosht (Zoroaster) to honor all of his commitments, no matter if those commitments were made to an honest or dishonest person. Mehr is present everywhere and hears those seeking his assistance. People who lie, cheat, or steal, experience a terrible life. Mehr is believed to have vast pasturelands, 1000 ears, and 10,000 eyes. People who keep their commitments are rewarded with abundance of happiness and helpful friends.

Mehregaan: This festival is in the honor of Mehr, and the victory of Fereidoon over Zah-haak. Mehregaan festival goes on for six days and people rest and take care of others who may need help. All rich people are encouraged to engage in acts of generosity by sharing their wealth with others in their community. Everyone is encouraged to take part in public works projects.

Norooz: The celebration marking the start of spring season.

Oppression: Abuse of authority and power to subdue and deny justice to people.

Peacock color cow: A mythical cow that provided rich milk to Fereidoon when he was a child.

Peerooz: Victory. In this context, it refers to overcoming one's own arrogance, and remembering to remain humble and mindful of the impact of one's deeds on others. The story of Jamsheed provides a constant reminder of what happens when arrogance is not kept in check. A common greeting during Norooz (New Year) is "Noroozetaan Peerooz!" This implies, May you be victorious in overcoming all internal and external obstacles during the New Year.

Persuaded audience: Roger Soder builds on the ideas of Ralph Lerner to distinguish between the concepts of *persuaded audience* and *thoughtful public*. In this context, a persuaded audience is assumed to be passive and often fooled by politicians. In contrast, a thoughtful public has many attributes and among them are: (1) has a sense of community, (2) cares for the general welfare, and (3) is alert. Soder argues we each have a role in choosing and supporting our political leaders. For a closer review of his arguments, please see the reference section for Soder's book: *The Language of Leadership*.

Ring: A symbolic circle that shows the commitment among the parties involved. Typically, we see the ring is held by a king. This shows the divine blessing has been bestowed upon a king to uphold public trust and defend their rights and interests.

Sepahbod = Army Chief.

Sormeh = Eyeliner: Used as cosmetics around the eyes.

Tahmoores: Mentioned in Avestaa as Tokhma Oropa. Known as Tahmoores-e deev-band (Tahmoores the one who roped the evil doers), for his bravery in fighting and defeating the people that attacked Iran. Tahmoores achieved his victory on the day of Khordaad and month of Farvardeen (6th of Norooz). According to the Iranian calendar Zoroastrians continue to use, each month has 30 days, and each day is named for an important element (e.g., fire, water, earth, wind, etc.) or a concept useful in building a productive society (e.g., peace, good thoughts, hard work, best truth, perfection, etc.)

Unum: Part of the Latin phrase, "E Pluribus Unum," which means, *out of many one*. The complete phrase shows the inherent tensions between unity and diversity in multicultural and democratic societies. If unity is over emphasized, then individual differences would disappear and can lead to tyranny of the majority. On the other hand, if diversity is over emphasized, then society could fragment and lead to isolated communities.

MEHREGAAN: THE TRIUMPH OF LIBERTY OVER TYRANNY

King Jamsheed:

During my reign of 70 years, Peace, prosperity, laughter and cheers!
I taught many things to all my peers. Melted iron for shields and made spears.
Wheels of progress turned all gears, People never felt sadness or fears!

Weaving and sowing, making fine clothes, Making bricks for walls, geometry shows!
Treating illnesses with fine medicine, Inventing good things, like Thomas Edison!
Nobody ever died of any illnesses, Singing and dancing were my witnesses!
Built new ships to sail the seas, Exporting progress with every breeze!

Brought new order to society, Distinct groups with notoriety.
Organized them all based on this list: Farmer, warrior, merchant, priest.
Everybody took care of one another, Children respected their father and mother.

When despaired people said: "Impossible!" I showed them progress truly possible!
I showed them that yes, they always can, Even fly high, just like the birdman!
Ring of commitment, solid and strong! People said to me, praises in a song.

Start of spring, celebrated Norooz!
Wished them all Victory: "Noroozetoon Peerooz!"
I failed a big test, couldn't be humble,
My arrogance grew, did not crumble!
Egotism, greed, not good! Agreed?
Forgiveness and love are what we need.

Unfortunately, I failed this time. My ego prevailed, ended peacetime.
Wars broke out, everywhere I looked, It was arrogance I had overlooked!
I claimed to have done it all my way, I lost it all, childish play!
Divine Grace left me soon after, Order collapsing, chaos thereafter.
Divine Blessing said a long "Goodbye!" For years, I've been asking myself, "Why?!"
My day became dark like a night. Anxiety, fears, with no delight.
Lost the crown and my throne, Who's to blame? All my own!

Farmer: What's happening to our king?
Why nobody wants to sing?
He used to be humble, kind.
The best king you'd ever find.

Together we all worked so well,
See the future and foretell,
What's happening to our king?
I see cracks in the ring!

Merchant: I don't like his attitude.
Something happened to his mood.
Crown too lofty for his head,
I am worried what's ahead.

Farmer: Careful friend of what you say!
Free speech has gone away.
You shouldn't say things so loud,
I also see dark cloud.

Metalsmith Kaaveh: I agree with both of you!
He's not the same king we knew.
He can't tell what's false or true,
Together we see it through.

Soldier: I was willing to follow
To high mountains, low meadow,
King's statements ring hollow,
Can't serve him with my longbow.

Father Time: Meanwhile news of unrest,
Made the king feel so depressed.
He knew his rule would end soon,
People hearing a different tune.

An evil king, but strong,
Azhidahaak, a bad song,
On right shoulder one snake,
Hard to believe, was it fake?!
On left shoulder another one,
Ugly snakes! Two, not one!
Three heads, three mouths, and six eyes!
"We've heard of him!" said spies!

King Jamsheed:
I can't believe this, people don't want me.
Tell me more about this crazy man,

What do I do now? Fight or hide, or flee?
How it all began, tell me his plan!

Advisor: Our good neighbor in southwest,
Killed his father to be king,
Young man with low self-esteem,
To have power, sold his soul,
Set a trap, dug a hole,

Son of Mardaas, man of zest,
Terror and shame he will bring.
Fell easy to evil's scheme.
Father's crown was his goal.
Mardaas fell in the sinkhole.

Azhidahaak seized his father's throne,
Devil changed into an expert cook,
Turned the king into a meat lover,
Nothing wanted from the king,
King wanted to reward him,
Kissed the king's shoulders, getting bolder,
All of a sudden, chef disappeared!

Called himself king, an evil seed sown.
He was nothing but a crook.
Acting always undercover.
Except his soul and everything!
Granted his wish on a whim.
Rubbed his eyes and face on King's shoulder.
Everybody said, "Wow! That's weird!!!"

Two snakes grew where the chef had kissed,
Frightened the king, with every twist,
Doctors were helpless, they had no cure!
King depressed, he had to endure!
One day devil came, as a physician,
Strange remedy, he had a mission.
"To kill the snakes, feed them two brains.
They leave you alone, you will have no pains."
Daily recipe, to wipe out man,
With this formula, devil's work began.

King did as was told, without much thinking,
He was just trapped, ever more sinking!

We use our brain to make decisions.
Young people build now and tomorrow.

When things go wrong, making revisions.
Wisdom of old, useful if you know.

Father Time: King Jamsheed was losing support,
Most people were leaving his court.
His arrogance turning them off,
They saw Zah-haak as a trade-off.

He was something totally new,
On his shoulders snakes grew.
Without thinking, people went to him,
People didn't know they'd lose a limb.
He ruled Iran for one thousand years,
Minus a day – fears and tears!
People wanted strong protector,
Not an evil brain collector.
People trapped in his scheme,
All they could do was scream!
Devil's plan was working for now,
Death everywhere was lurking somehow.

Brain was the snake food,
The royal chefs did all they could,
Replacing one man with just one sheep,
Saving just one man, life's not cheap!
This was the chef's daily routine,
Feeding snakes, an ugly scene.
Snakes were fooled, they remained quiet,
People were not fooled, they learned the diet.
When people gave up their rational mind,
They showed ignorance of all mankind.
What's the lesson? Following fools,
Gets you nowhere! Brains are tools.

Farmer: I don't like this king, scary Oppressor!
Forget enemies, he is the aggressor!
No legitimacy, has no honor!
Sooner or later, he is a goner!

Merchant: I lost two sons to his snakes,
My tears have filled many, many lakes.
I'm done crying, I have what it takes,
Get rid of him, put on him the brakes!

Metalsmith Kaaveh: Yesterday, Zah-haak's soldiers barged into my house!
Took away our son, they hurt my spouse!
We are fed up with this ruler so evil,
We are ready for change, a major upheaval!

Farmer: Have you heard the news today?
King has something he wants to say,
At his palace is a show,
Wants to gloat and glow.

Metalsmith Kaaveh: I will go to court, say to his face,
You're an evil king, major disgrace!
What will it take for us to completely erase,
Your harm and madness from this place?

Farmer: Be careful not to offend,
I tell you as a friend.
His soldiers are everywhere,
Causing fear and despair!

Metalsmith Kaaveh: To the sun, I do swear,
With every breath of fresh air,
I say to you my good friends,
Let us begin new trends,
Injustice must end now!
We the people, can't allow,
Our youth to be killed by him
Hope of future is so dim!

Father Time: Resentment to Zah-haak's rule,
Grew every day, he was cruel.
40 years before losing his throne,
He had a dream, future was shown.
He saw a young man, wielding a bull mace,
Coming after him, taking his place.
He was frightened, his days were numbered.
Tried changing tide, he was outnumbered.

Summoned advisors, all were scared,
Told them his nightmare, notes they compared.
Fereidoon will come, seize your throne,
We are your subjects, you're not alone.
Send your spies now everywhere you can,
Look for Fereidoon, young child not old man!
Seize all the babies, spare no clan,
Don't let him escape! This is the plan!

Zah-haak's soldiers searched every land,
Ended many lives, all sons were banned.
Fereidoon's father, Aabteen his name,
Killed by the king, O what a shame!
He was from royal blood,
His son was just a flower bud.
Faraanak, his mom, took him away,
To a safe place, to grow, play.
Trusted a farmer, to raise her son,
Believing that good will be done!
Noble farmer lived near a mountain,
Peacock color cow, a milk fountain.
For three years, cared for the newborn son,
Hid him from harm, to grow and have fun.

Zah-haak's soldiers found out about him,
They killed the cow, and things were grim.
Faraanak again took her son away,
Left the country, lived another day.

Fereidoon was 16, becoming a man,
Came down the mountain, his journey began.
Asked his mother, about family's past,
"Why in our country, we live like outcast?!"

She told him about grandpa Tahmoores,
Was he fearless and cultured? Definitely, yes!
It was his turn to fight, make things right,
End the darkness, bring the bright light.
Honor, pride, justice for all,
When we join forces, dictator will fall.

Zah-haak: I asked you all to come here,
Listen to me with your ear.
I feel a secret enemy,
Even you may be frenemy,
Will do me harm, given a chance,
How can I know your true stance?
My military commander,
Will lead this task with candor.
This is a survival fight,
It's all about might, not right!

Advisor: Your Majesty, your throne is protected,
We have a plan, mistakes corrected.
Let us invite people here,
To see you, respect, and fear,
Sign a pledge, show their respect,
Commit to you as loyal subject.

Every corner an armed guard,
Spies even in the yard,
People show their loyalty,
We'll punish any disloyalty.

Zah-haak: Send messengers everywhere,
Tell people come, and beware,
I'll know who came to greet me,
I may hear their plea.

نشان فریدون بگرد جهان   همی باز جست آشکار و نهان
Looked for signs of Fereidoon all over the world,
Searched where he could see, even hidden world.

Father Time: Palace doors, wide open.
People's spirits, broken.
Time to meet and greet the king,
It felt like a bee sting!
People paraded before him,
Festivities were grim.
Guards were watching everyone,
A fearful time, not so fun!
Like sheep many signed the pledge,
Everybody was on edge.
Zah-haak pleased with charade,
A gentle face was portrayed.
People had their heads down low,
They were going with the flow.

Sepahbod/Military Commander: Come forward and show respect,
You understand me, correct?!
Sign this oath of loyalty,
In presence of royalty.

Metalsmith Kaaveh: Before I sign anything,
I want to tell you something.
You claim to be a just king,
When will your justice begin?
Why you took my son away?
He was at home yesterday.
He hasn't done any harm,
He is a young man with charm!
What's your excuse for cruelty?
Your snakes aren't beauty!
Are you a king or dragon?
Judgment someday will happen!

Sepahbod/Military Commander: Who are you and what you want?
You are what you do flaunt!
Tell me again, who you are,
Where do you work in bazaar?

Metalsmith Kaaveh: I work daily with metal,
I have a dispute to settle.
I bend metal and twist,
Injustice, I will resist.

Your soldiers came seized my son,
In my home I'm overrun.
To feed his snakes, he's my son!
Which side are you, hired gun!
Is this justice in your books?
Is this how your justice looks?

Sepahbod/Military Commander:
You made me think about my role,
Not sure why I'm doing this,

Release this man's son to him!
Once returned he may say,

Frankly, I am most shocked!
This man has guts, not afraid,

I am confused, who am I?
He made me think, and ask why,

In his game I'm a pawn.
I am a man of people,

Have I also lost my soul?
Tired of his snakes' hiss!

I am acting on a whim,
"All forgiven! Praises, pray!"

Path to victory is blocked.
With fire he always played.

Kaaveh's story is not lie!
Work for a monster-six-eye!

Do you see me as a con?
I am sensing upheaval.

Metalsmith Kaaveh:
Expecting me sign a false letter?!
Your king kills us in cold blood,

Good kings bring peace and wealth,
Ring of commitment is lost.

My pledge is to the sun,
This letter I rip in half,

Taking a stand is hard,
Final stop, graveyard.

Since when you say lying is better?
The day he falls, we'll hear a thud.

They improve public health.
Signing letter, at what cost?!

Path of truth is the one!
To teach my son and your staff.

In life, we should be on guard!
Meantime, play your best card!

Advisor: Now that you did let him go,
Kingly gesture, we all know.
Will give others courage though,
Fereidoon winds will blow!

I was amazed what I heard,
Kaaveh was like thunderbird!
He certainly has stirred,
Emotions not seen or heard!

Father Time: Kaaveh walked out with his son,
Shaken, proud, yelled "we won!"
"Rise up people, see the sun!"
"We want Fereidoon!" said someone.

Committed to get the job done,
People joined him one by one,
The movement had just begun,
Fighting darkness with the sun!

Fereidoon heard his name called out,
People wanted him, no doubt!
To claim the throne, in justice!
To end era of injustice!

Father Time: Put his apron on a lance, Rallied people to advance,
Never looking back, no glance, He was taking a big chance!

People added jewels and gold, Precious stones many fold,
Yellow, purple, red and white, Beautiful flag, what a sight!

   Kaviani flag (Derafsh-e Kaaveeyaanee), it was named,
     Justice, Freedom it claimed.
That cheap apron was transformed,   Worthy symbol that informed:
    We the people want justice,
     We are against injustice!
    We choose our own good leaders,
    When we find them, they're keepers!
    We want them sane and honest,
     Expect good things they promised.
   We support freedom of expression,
     Inquiry good, ask question!
    Trust, respect for a just law,
     Equal justice under the law.
   Thoughtful public wants leaders,
     Accountable, no cheaters!
  Persuaded audience don't look deep,
    Often they are led like sheep.
     Order is not oppression,
     Freedom is not aggression.
     We the people are many,
     "unum" is made of many!

Mehr was watching in the sky, He was also their ally.
He heard and saw everything, He was the one with the ring!
His arrows aimed at the foe, Keep promises, high or low.
Honest people call his name, Mehr always helps, with sharp aim!
His castle is in the sky, His chariot can fly!
Mehr comes always with the light, Brings victory and delight!

Fereidoon: I am here to join you all,
Eager, proud, standing tall!
We owe Kaaveh a great deal,
We hope someday our wounds heal.
Let's all unite for this fight,
Morning will come after night.
Thank you for this bull-head mace,
Humbly seeking Mehr's grace!
My dad, Aabteen, will be proud,
See me with you, enlightened crowd.

Kaaveh: We the people are sovereign,
Dragon's place is coffin.
We need to fight him often,
With heat, metal will soften.

Solider: My weapons will serve honest folks,
Wrap the dragon with some ropes.
Honor to be with you all,
My honor restored with this call!
I will side with my comrades,
With you mothers, and you dads!
You have suffered so much so,
This dragon is our foe!

Merchant: I've bought and sold many things,
Carpets, clothes, even rings.
I've seen many poor, bad kings,
This monster, worst of all beings!
I'll never trade freedom!
I will rise up, I'm not numb.
I'll never accept Unfairness!
I have seen light of Awareness!

Father Time: Zah-haak on the run,
His forces overrun.
Fereidoon hot on his trail,
Zah-haak getting frail.
Zah-haak out of tricks,
No more politics.

Mount Damaavand, site of last stand.
Fighting was over, Zah-haak lost command!
Three heads, three mouths, and six eyes!
"We've captured him!" He was the prize!

Zah-haak: 40 years ago, had a nightmare,
Your bull-head mace met my chair.
Losing my crown, what a rejection!
Seems like you won in this election!

Merchant: He should pay for his cruelty.
Now that we have fortuity,
He is guilty, no ambiguity!
Chance for justice, continuity!

Farmer: He deserves severe punishment,
See red tulips in the field,
The least would be banishment.
Remind us justice revealed.

Soldier: I will put him right in jail,
His snakes will go with him,
He won't get out, there is no bail.
Chance of getting out is dim!

Kaaveh: We should always remain alert!
Our right to have a just king!
Remind leaders we will assert,
Commitment must be solid ring!

Fereidoon: Zah-haak will stay in jail,
A lesson for all, young and old,
Our freedom, not for sale!
History repeats, we are told.

People deserve much better,
Liberty, justice are for all,
We all should work together.
Dictator caused his own fall.

To perfect our union,
Truth and justice must prevail,
Celebrate communion,
Trust and reason need no veil.

Fire of truth transparent,
People will serve the warrant,
We do not want a tyrant.
Create a moving current.

We believe in common good,
Teaching peace at childhood,
We are against all falsehood.
May stay through adulthood.

Fereidoon:
To honor our victory, Mark a day in history,
Let's rest today and reflect, With Mehr we all should connect.

Truth and justice do matter, Freedom is what we're after.
In life, you are an actor, Start today, new chapter.

Open the gates of treasury, Help all in need, end beggary.
Plant happy seeds, good memory, Legacy of our ancestry!

Zah-haak is jailed, we're free today! Analyze orders, before you obey!
Holding a red cup, sing and dance and play, Pausing to reflect, resting is okay!

Light the fire, praises to Mehr, He sees everyone with his stare!
Liars and cheaters, you'll have nightmares, Ring of commitment, social welfare.
The ruler commits to uphold the law, The people decide a fair bylaw.
The ruler commits to reason, truth! The people decide at the voting booth!

Father Time:
Mehr is also name of the seventh month, When evil is caught in a hunt.
The first month of fall season, Remembering to reason.
People wear their fine clothes, Want to strike a new pose.
Colorful table for fall colors, Consulting with wise scholars!

Wild marjoram in water, Smells so good, at altar.
Sormeh is called eyeliner, Making eyes look diviner.

Lotus, wild marjoram, and sugar plumb seeds,
A handful thrown over heads, good fortune feeds.
All the rituals, we don't know them all,
Life does go on, this season is fall.

A table set to honor Mehr, To show, people do really care!
Mirror bright, just like the sun, Vegetables, fruits, bazillion ton!
Gold coins to share, things to drink, Using our brain, to care, to think!
Candies, sweets, rosewater too, They are treats, just a few.

Pistachios, almonds are fine nuts, You can say the same for peanuts.
Pomegranates, apples fine fruits, Their red colors show, life in pursuits.

Father Time:

What happens when leaders become arrogant and ungrateful?
Why is it important to be rational and mindful?
Was Zah-haak's punishment fair?
What would you have done, if you were there?

What did you learn from this story?
Can you point to an allegory?
Myths are powerful like history.
They are living puzzles with mystery!

Examine images on this page,
Point to the one on stage,
You consider most vital,
Go ahead, give it a title.

Father Time: Zah-haak was jailed at Damaavand Mountain. His capture serves as a reminder to avoid dictators, and resist unchecked power.

Zah-haak (Azhidahaak) ruled Iran for one day short of 1000 years. Fereidoon replaced him and ruled Iran for 500 years. He was famous for his generosity and fair rule. He established the Mehregaan festival and shared wealth with others.

Iranians celebrate Mehregaan on Mehr day and month of Mehr. Mehregaan public festival begins on the 16th day of the seventh month. Festivities go on for six days, through Raam day (Tranquility). Families gather around the Mehregaan table and remember the events that happened on such a day. A few of the major events and past rituals are: (1) victory of Fereidoon over Azhidahaak; (2) heavenly deities coming to help Fereidoon; (3) at sunrise, a chosen brave guard calling on the heavenly deities to come and help people fight evil; (4) the last day of festivities is a private event marking the day Fereidoon's supporters jailed Zah-haak at Damaavand mountain. In other words, each person needs to think about how best to conduct himself or herself in order to protect the public good. (5) people receiving gifts from those who are well off; (6) sun was created and brightened the moon; (7) humans were created; (8) Mehr is not the sun, but rather, is the guardian of light and brightness; (9) before appearing at the Mehregaan table, people should wash and be clean. It is likely that this ritual went to Europe and became part of the rites of passage in Christianity. The mirror serves as portal to look deep into one's own heart and do what's right. Decorating the eyes with eyeliner (sormeh) is another symbolic ritual that shows the eyes are windows to our soul and like the sun enable us to see. Showing generosity is part of Mehregaan festival. Community members who have the means finance public works and other activities benefiting all.

Mehr is an Iranian Zoroastrian deity. According to Mehr Yasht, AhuraMazdaa told Zartosht (Zoroaster) to honor all of his commitments and contracts, no matter what. Mehr is believed to have 1,000 ears and 10,000 eyes. Mehr is always alert, seeing and hearing every person who honors or breaks promises. He is most strong and brave. Mehr has vast pasturelands. Mehr resides atop a high mountain (Alborz) that is bright and has a long chain of mountains. In this mythical place, there is no night, no cold wind, no hot wind, and no diseases. Mehr's path is always lit with bright lights and he supports honest people in their efforts to seek justice. Mehr cannot be deceived! He is an articulate speaker with a pleasant voice.

www.ingramcontent.com/pod-product-compliance
Lightning Source LLC
Chambersburg PA
CBHW060757090426

42736CB00002B/61